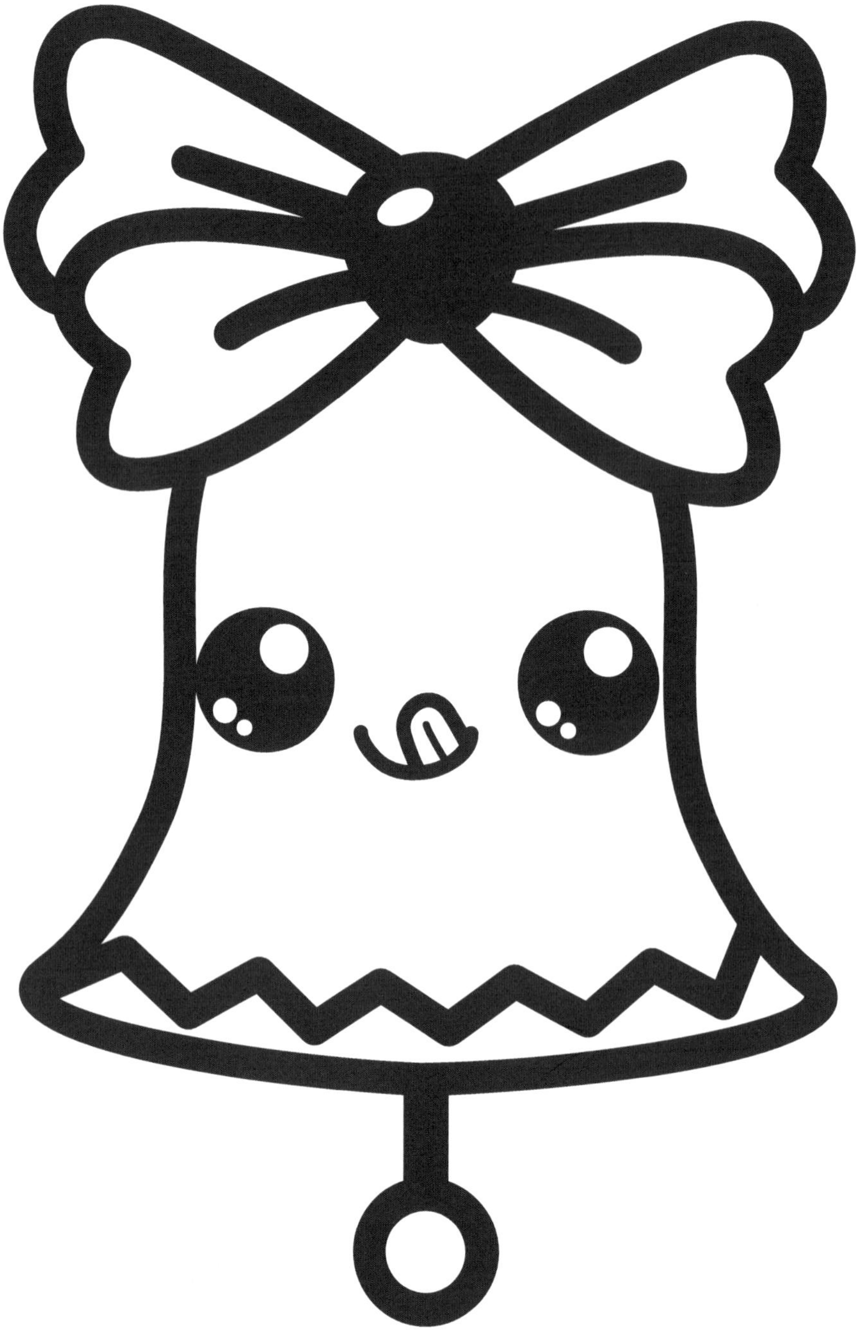

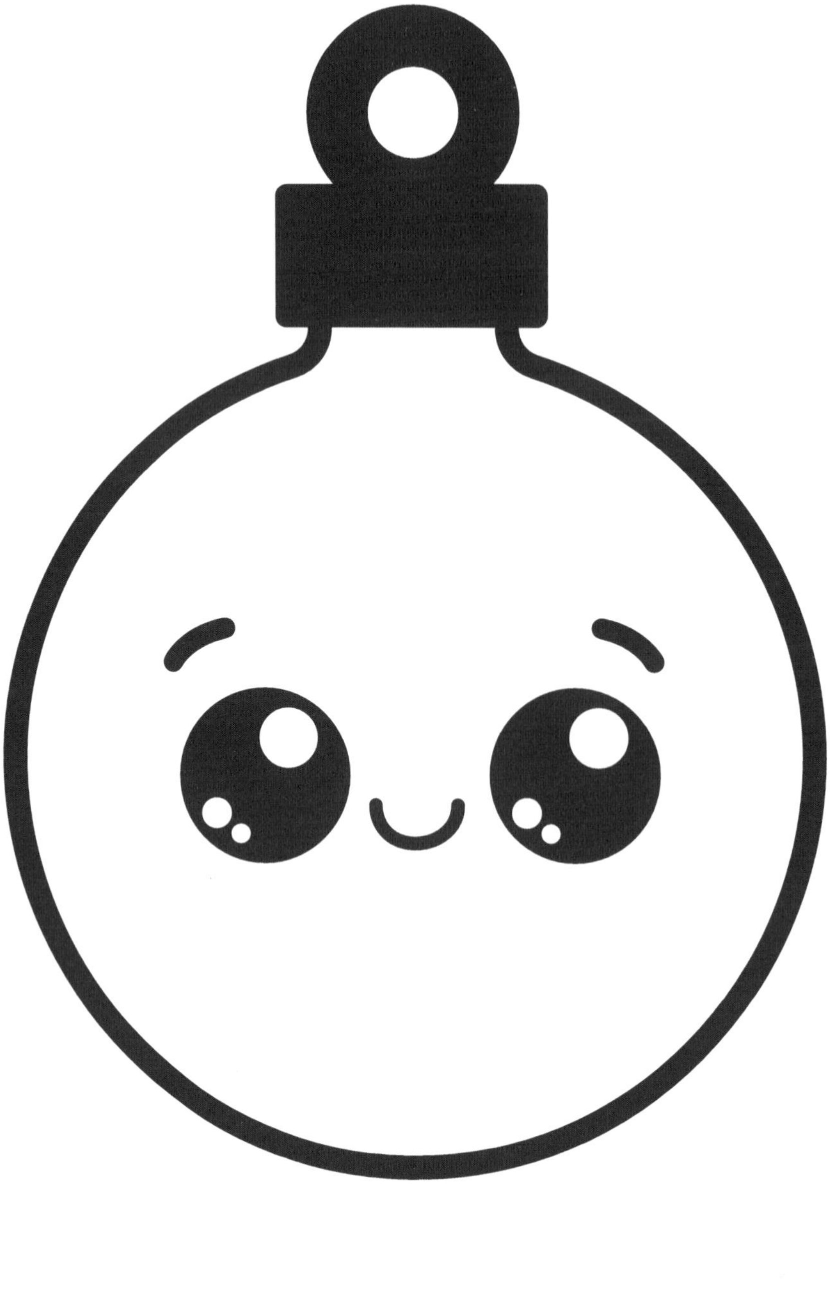

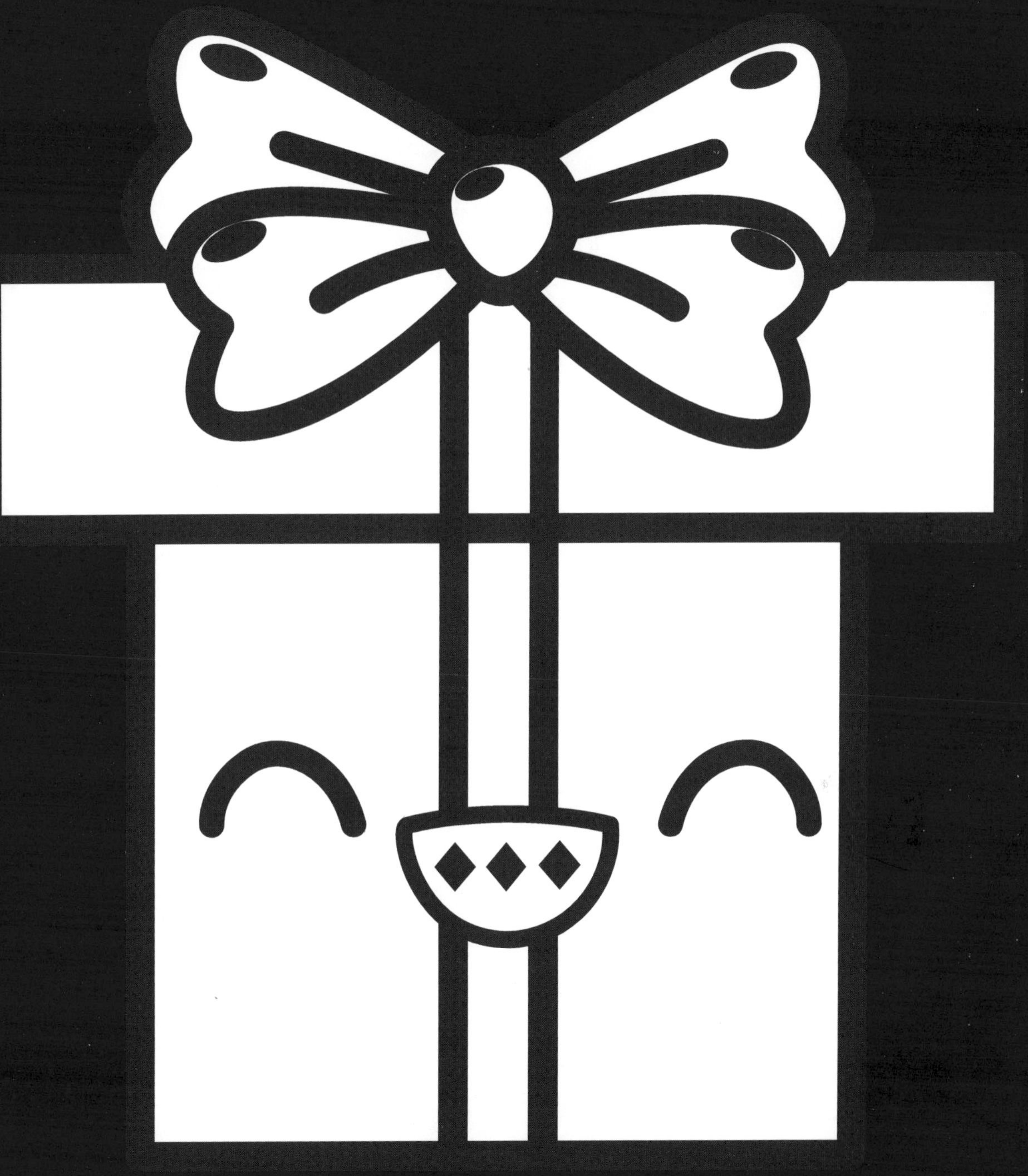

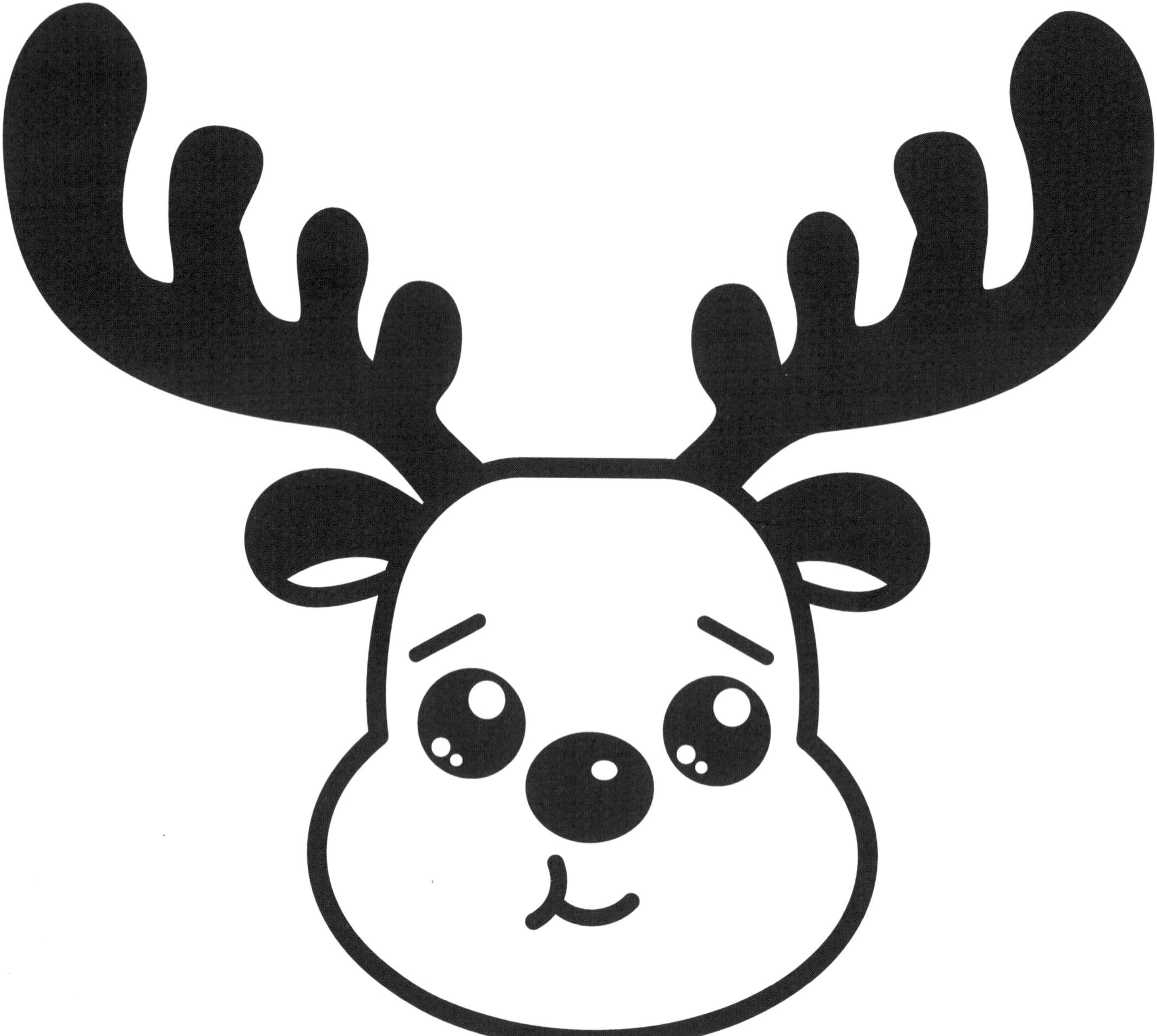

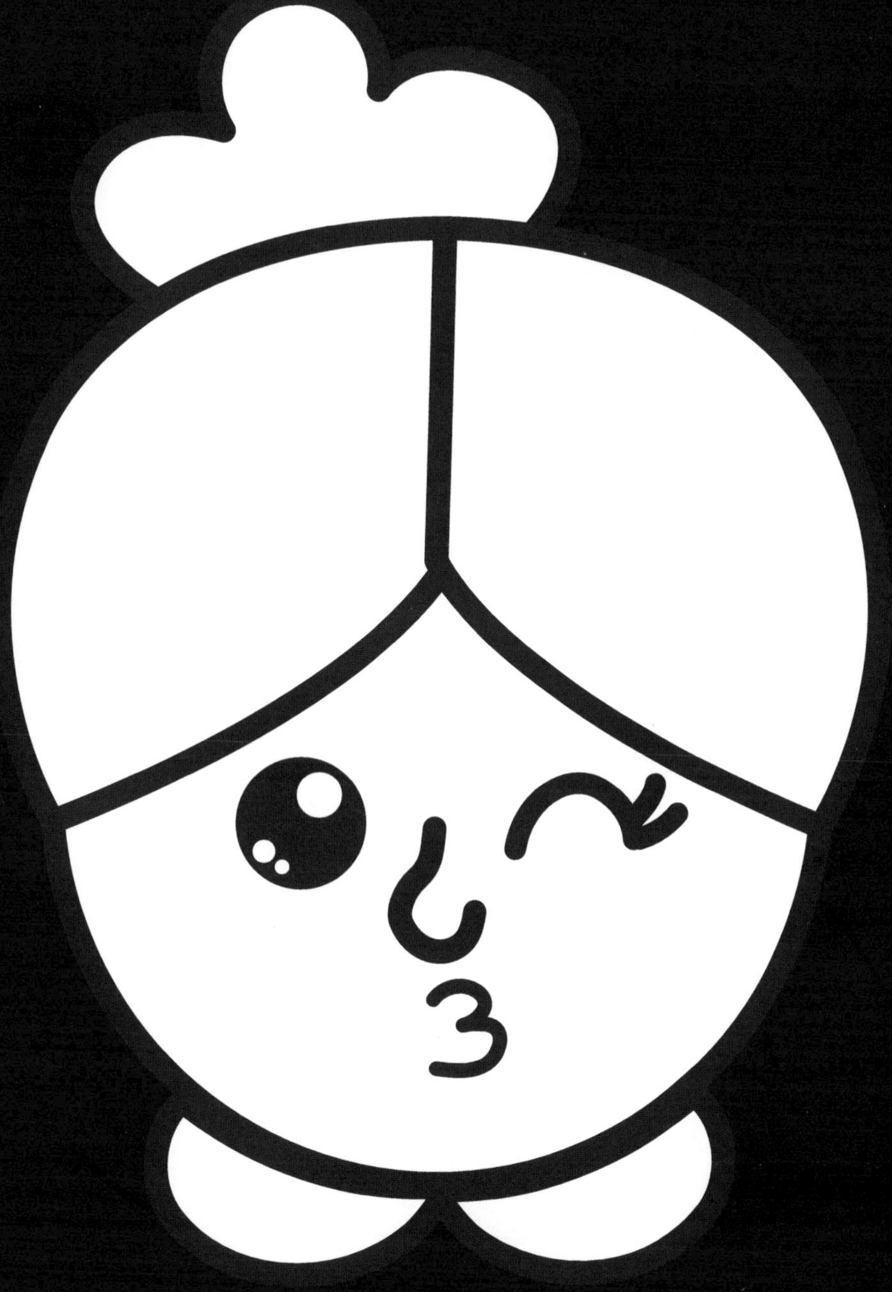

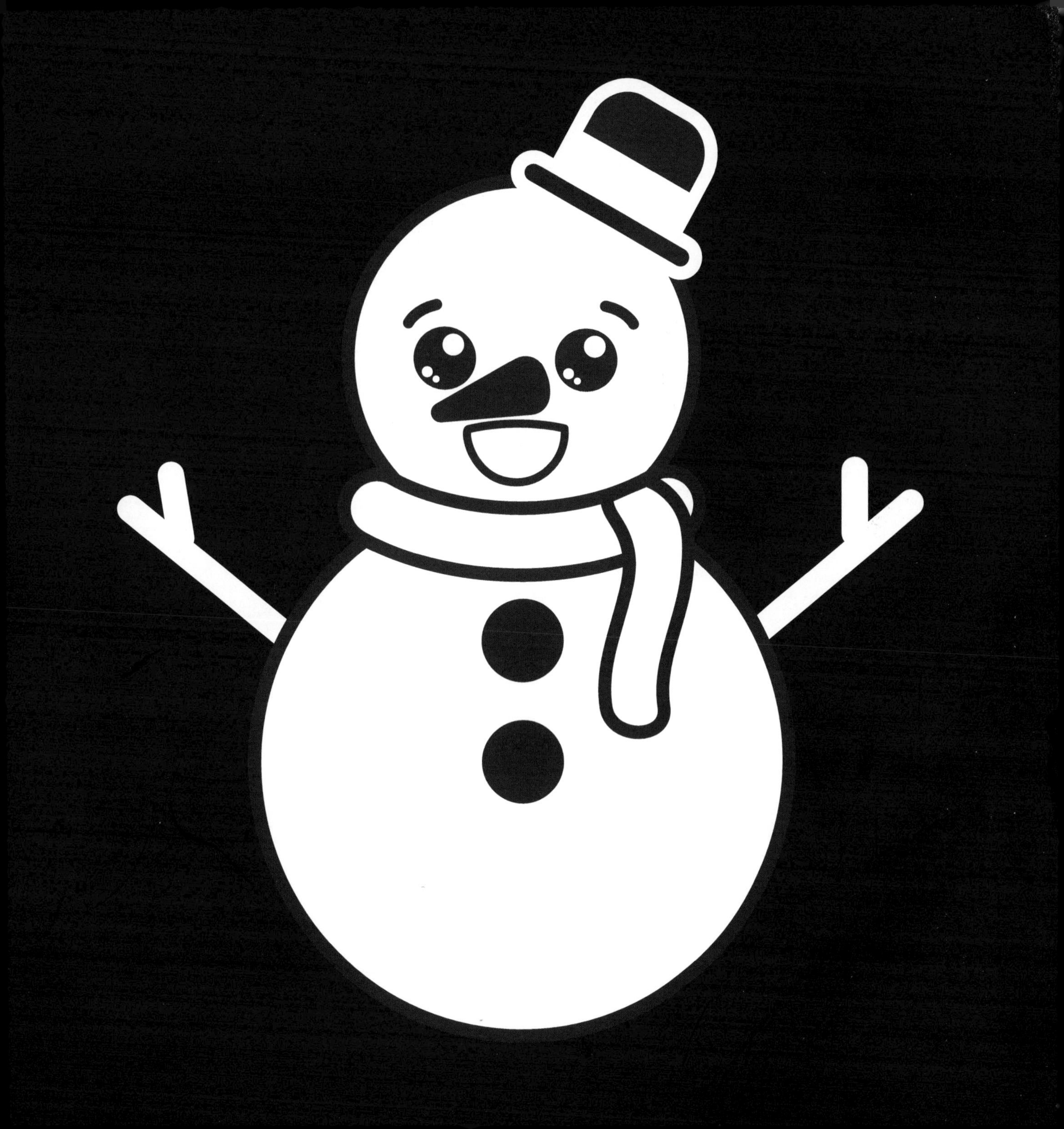

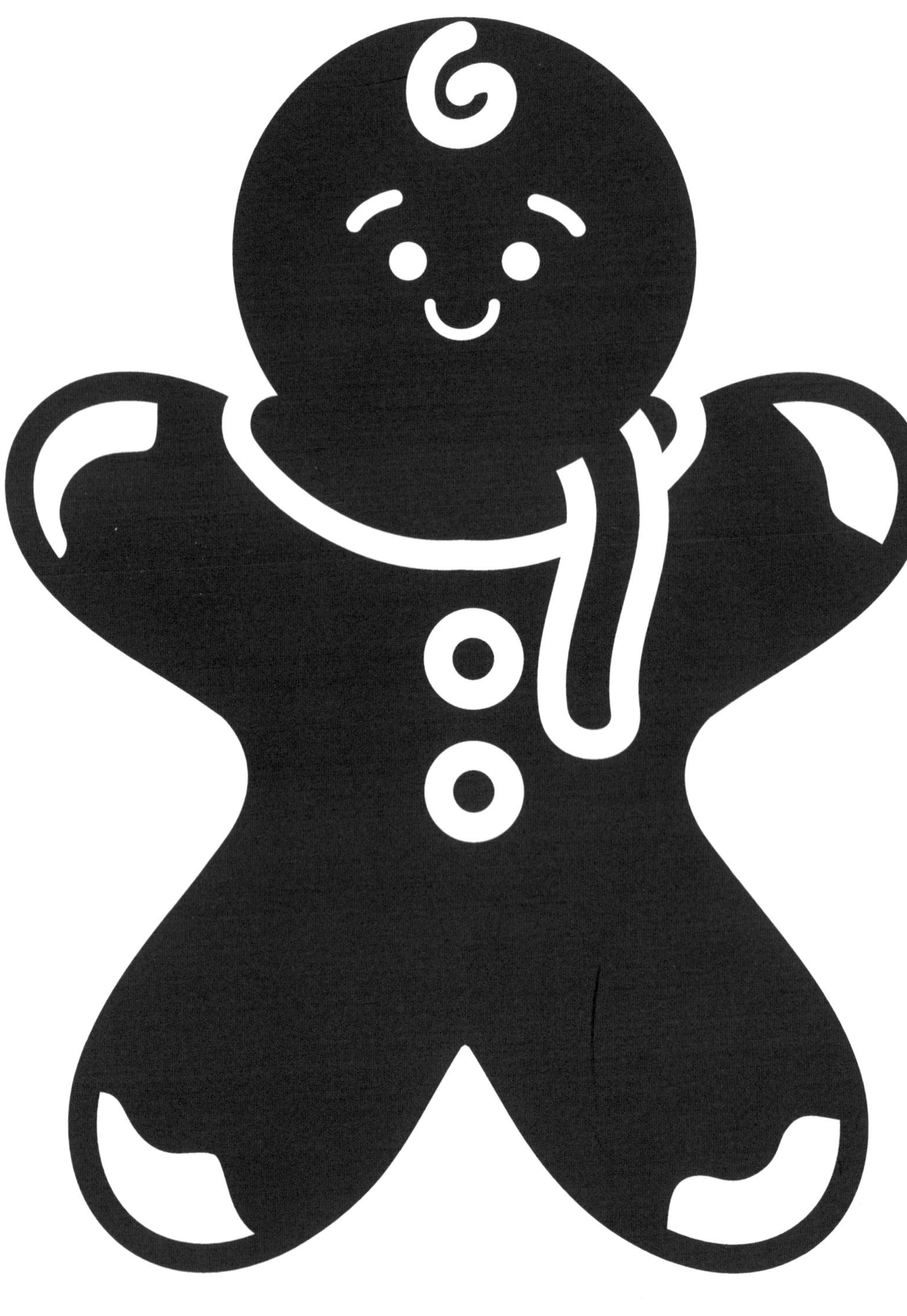

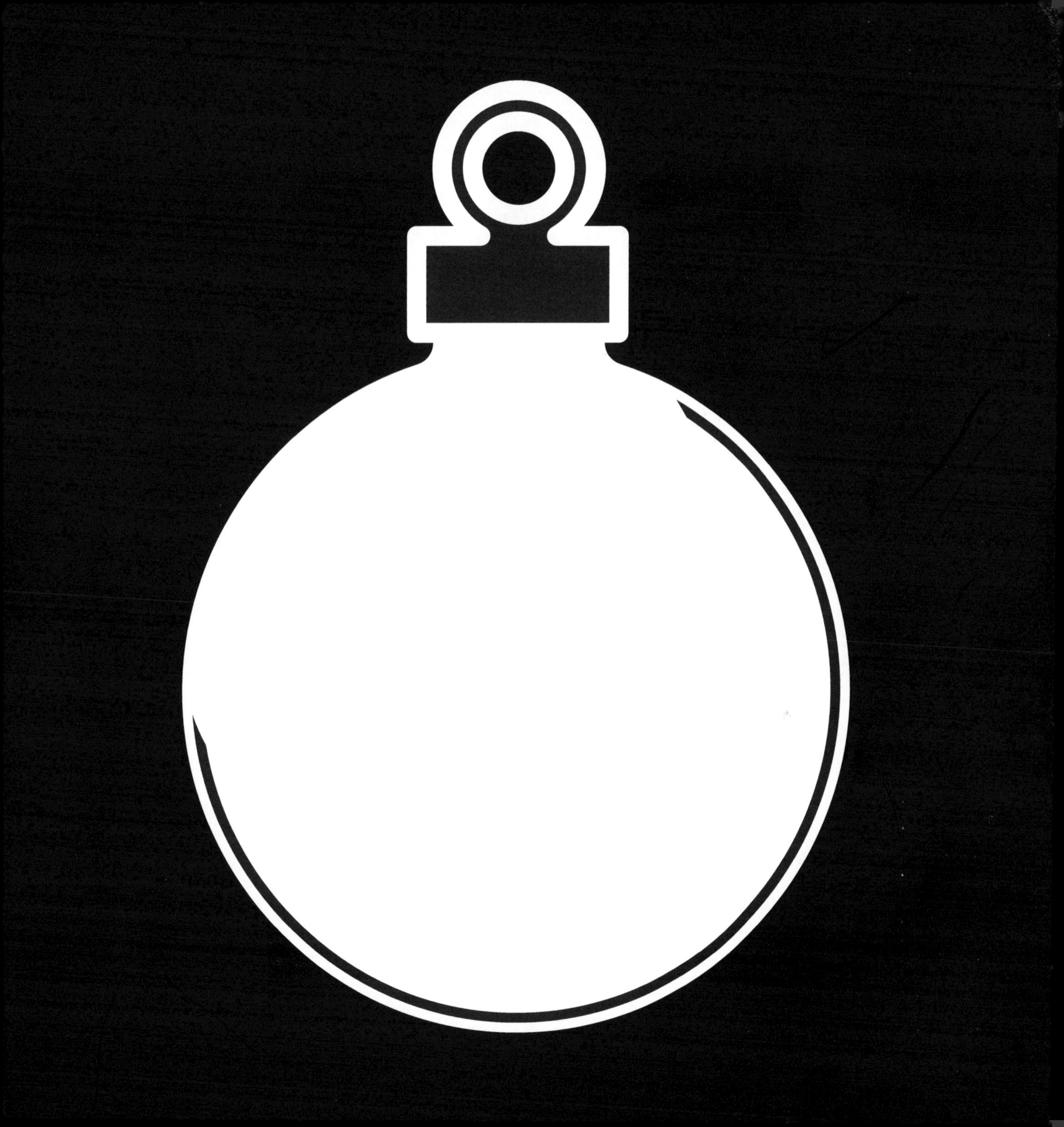

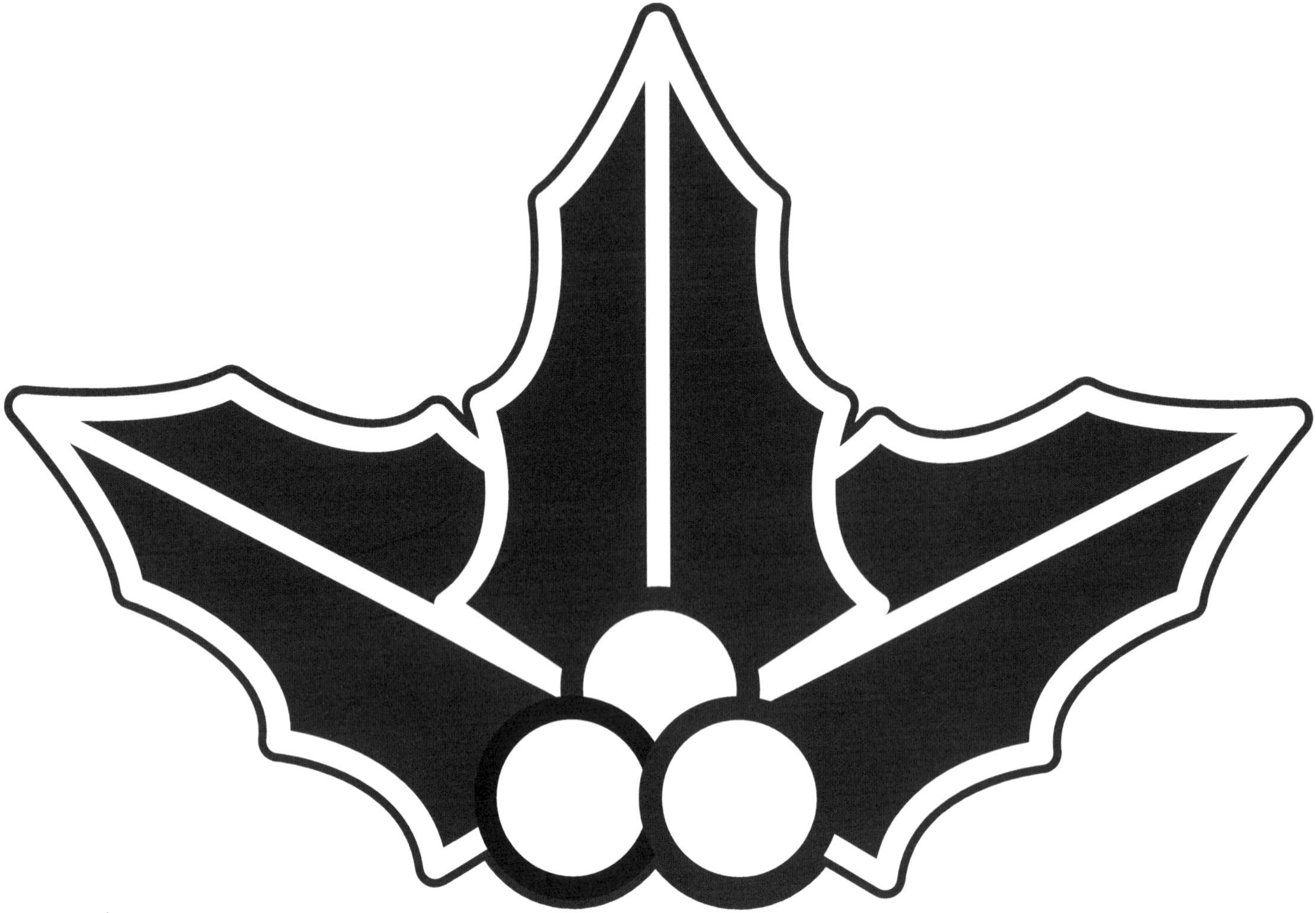

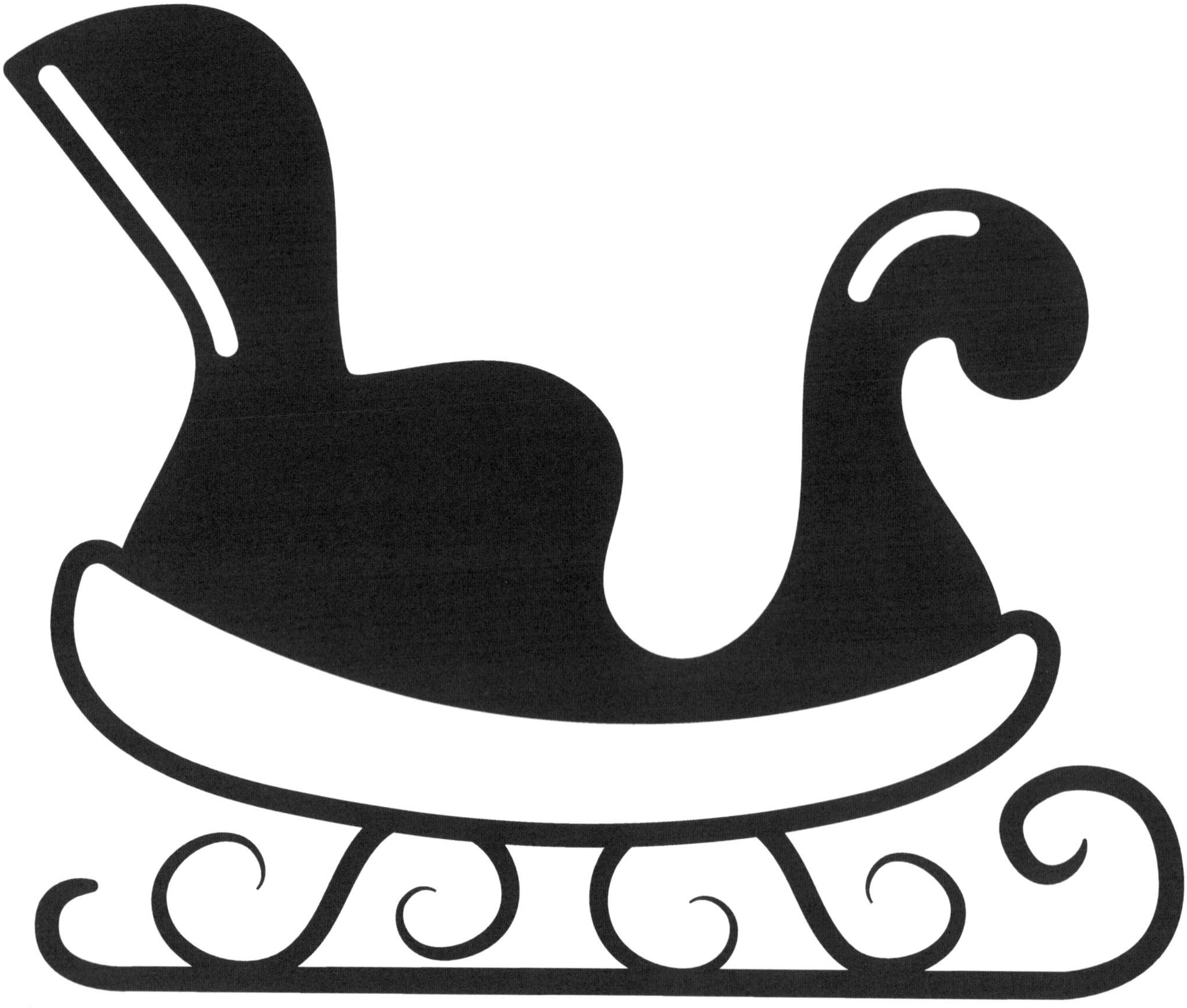

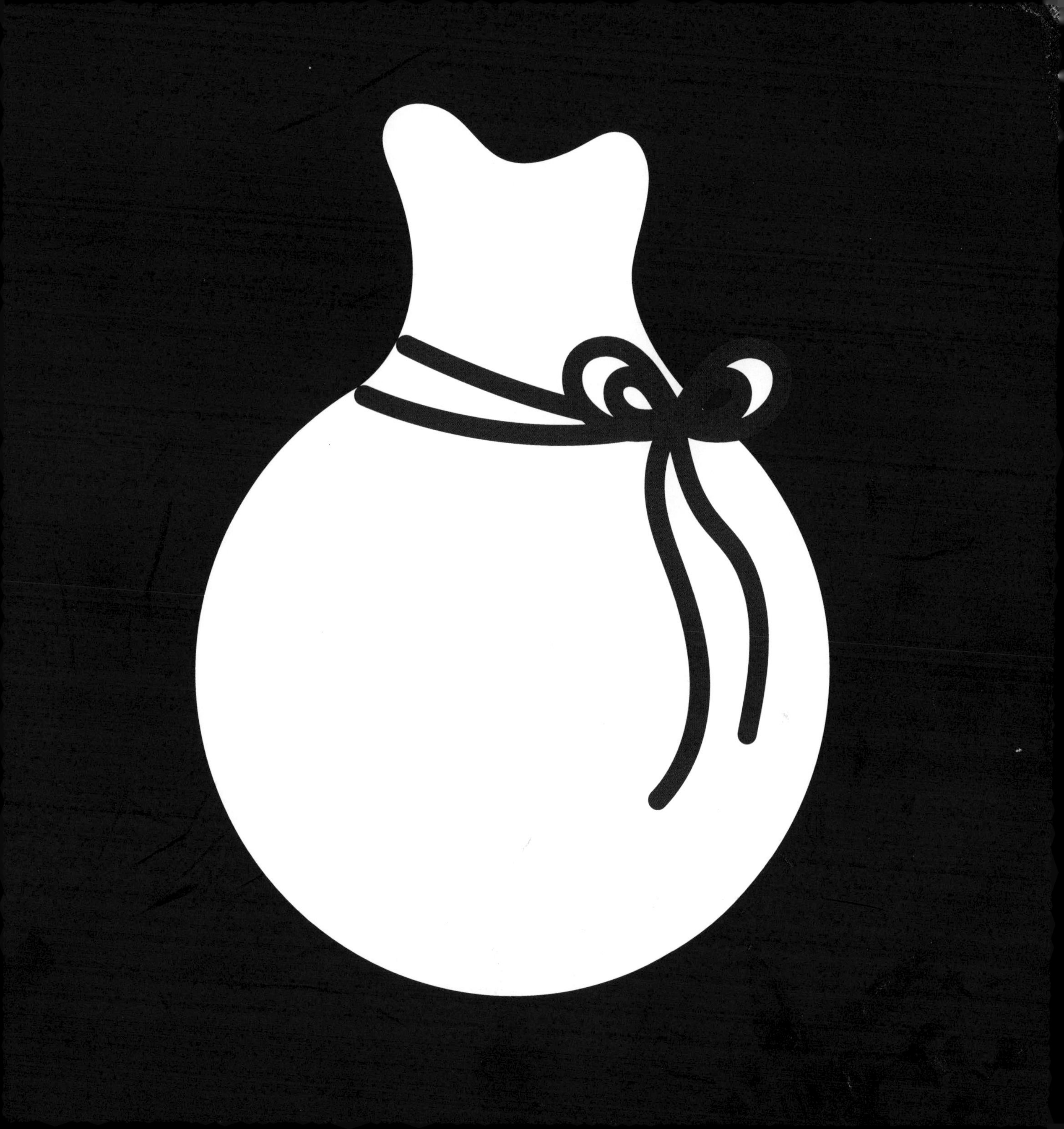

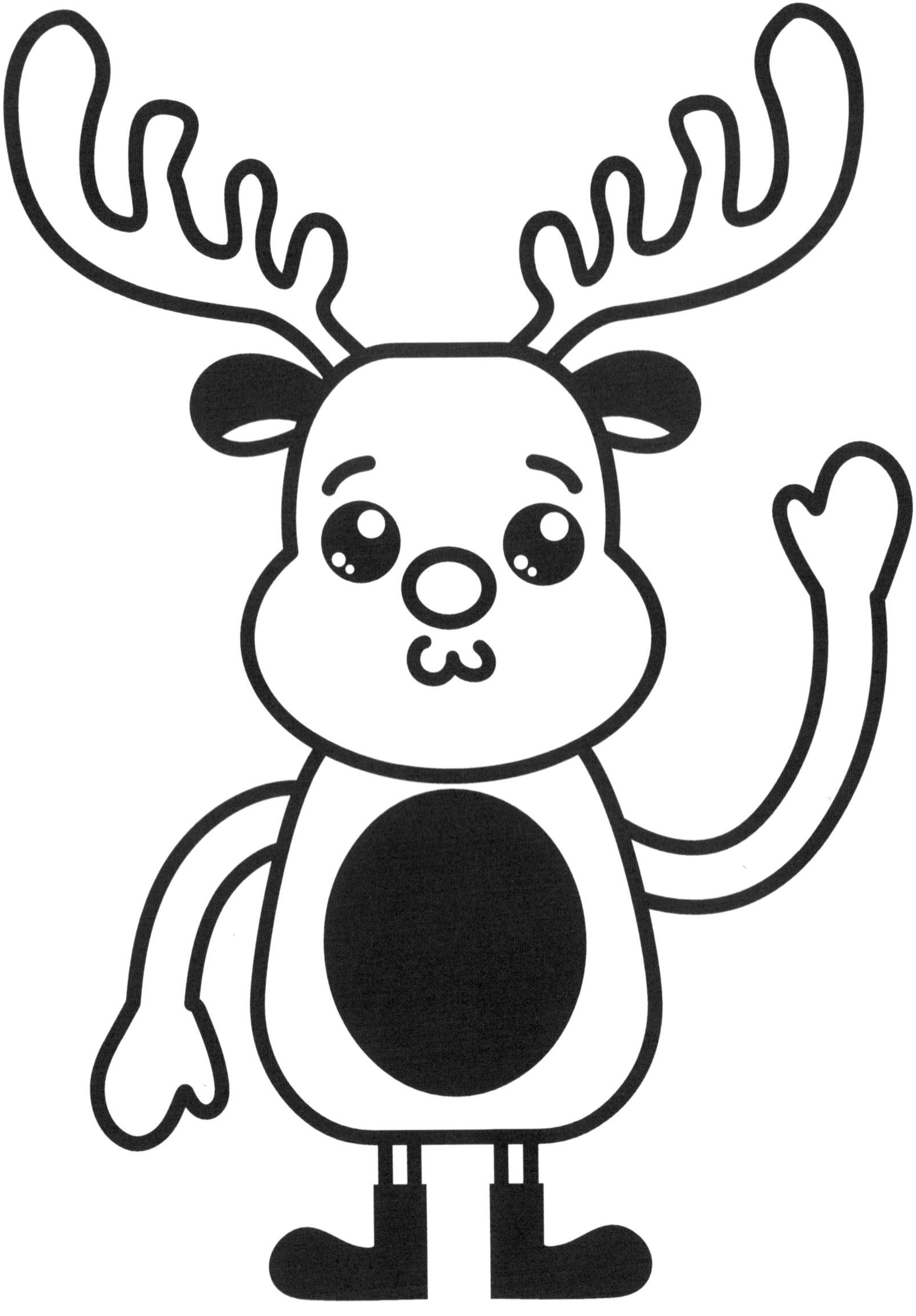

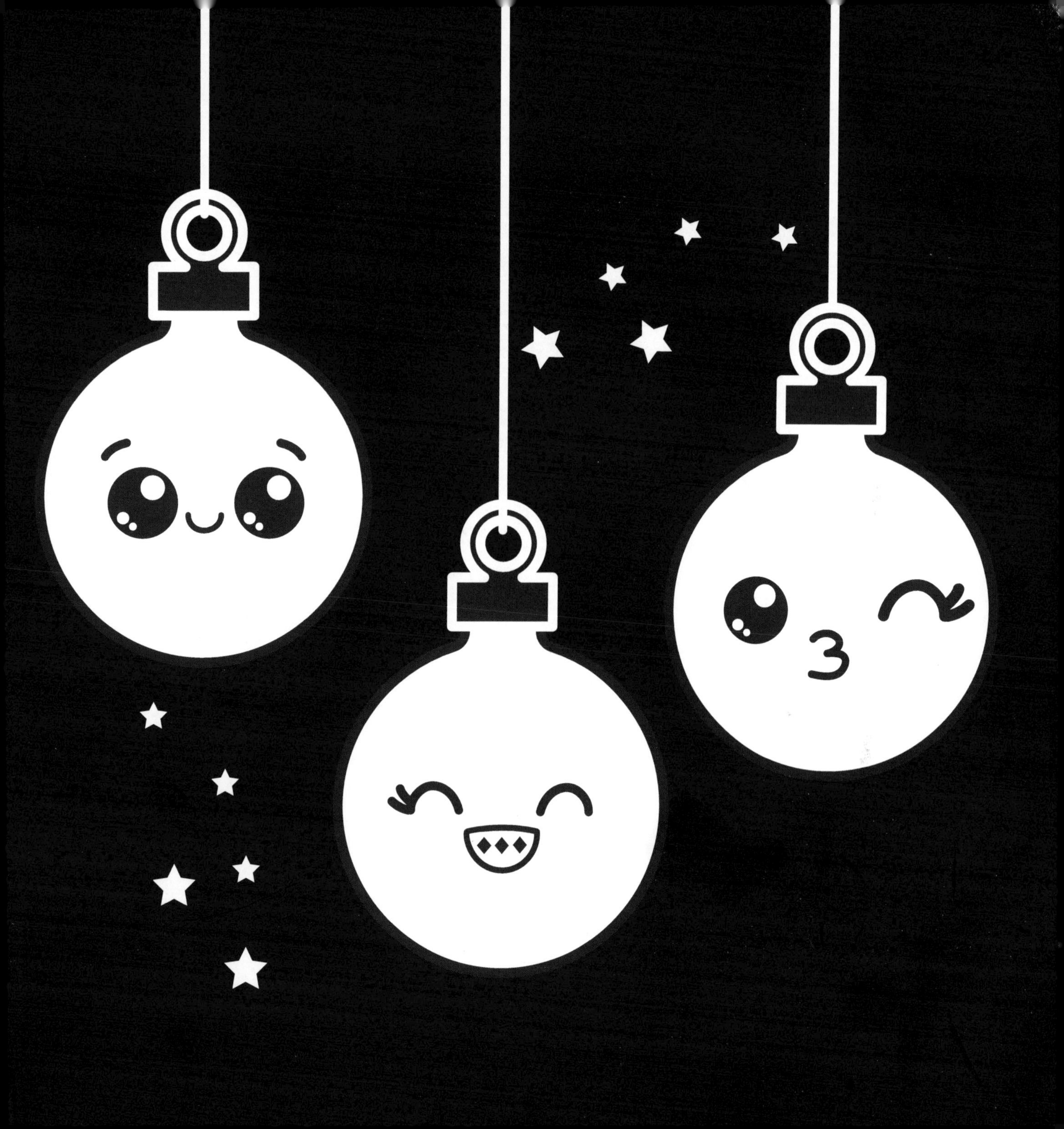

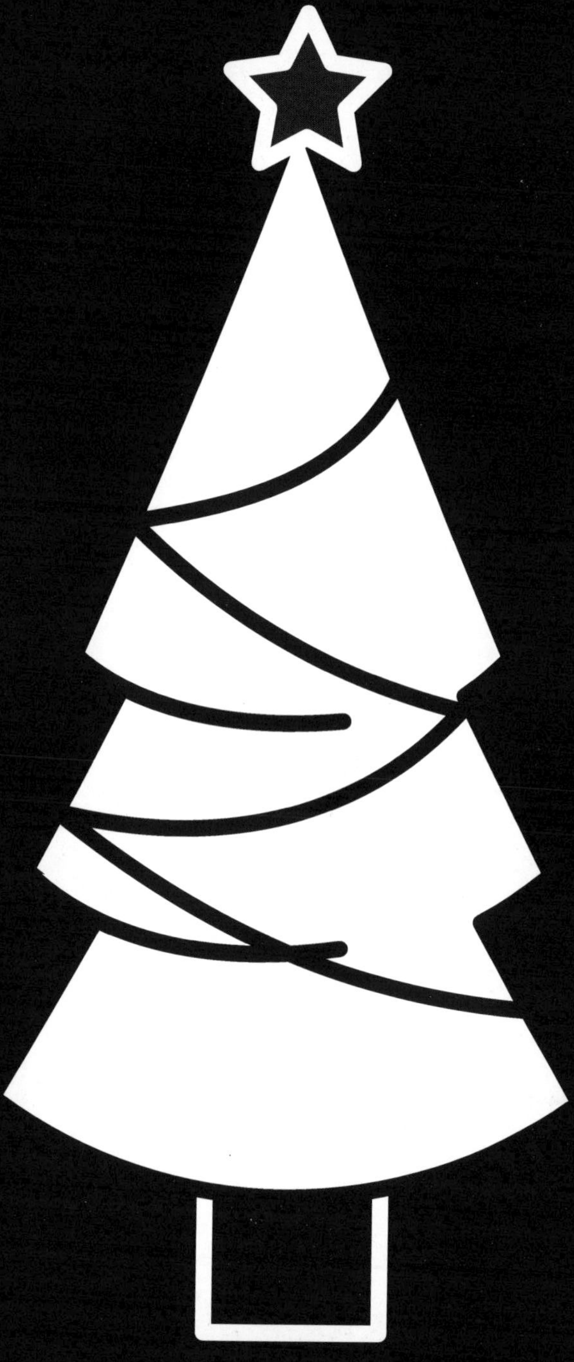

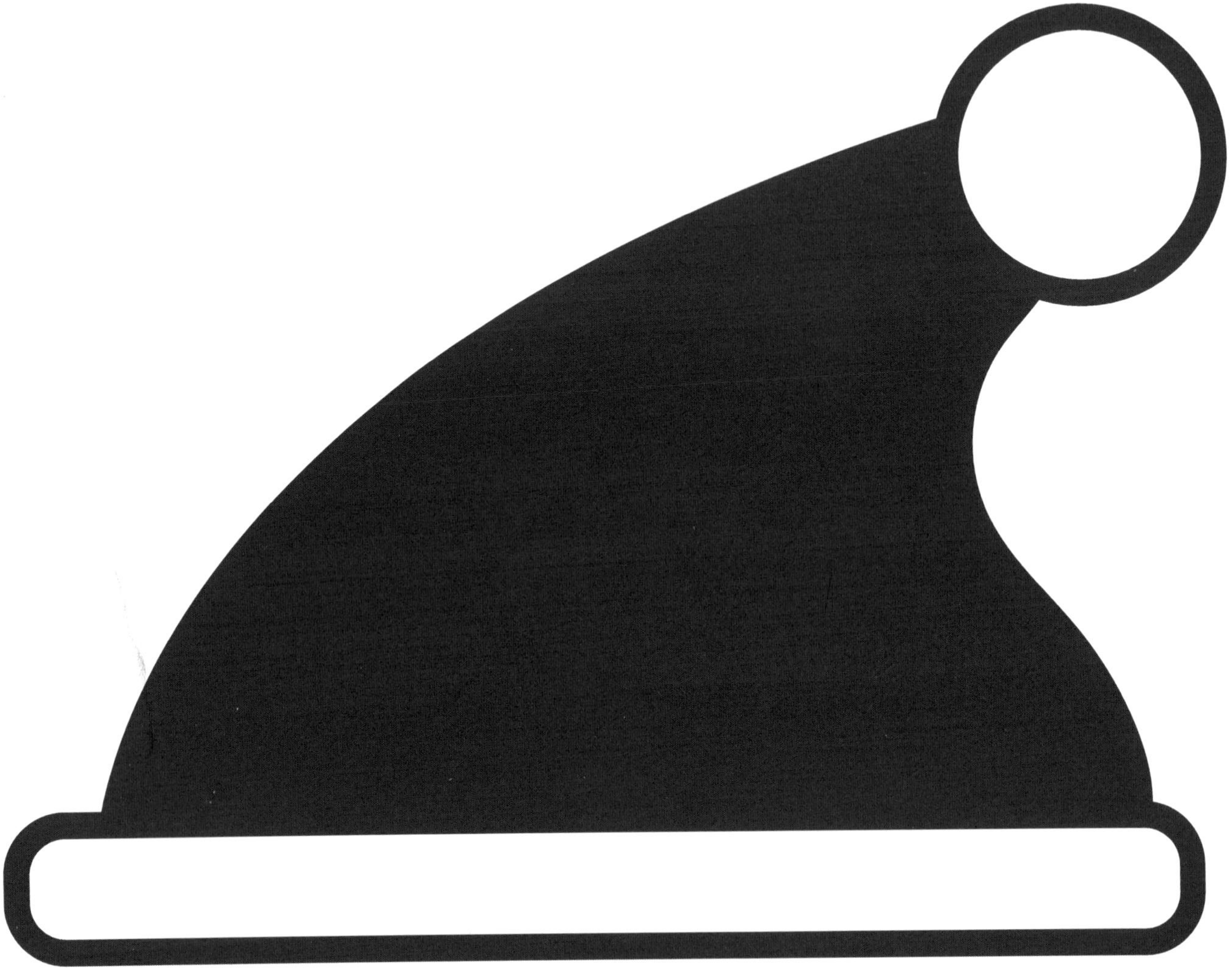

We'd love your feedback!

Like many other moms, you may have seen our book reviews. We invite you to add your voice to the conversation and share your experience with future buyers!

☺

Visit our website GreenOwlPress.com for freebies!

Printed in Great Britain
by Amazon